Edge of House

also by Dzvinia Orlowsky

A Handful of Bees

Edge of House

Dzvinia Orlowsky

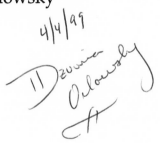

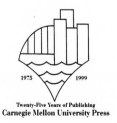

1975   1999

Twenty-Five Years of Publishing
Carnegie Mellon University Press

Acknowledgments

My thanks to the editors of the following magazines and journals, in which some of these poems first appeared, sometimes in different versions and under different titles:

Agni: Wieliczka Salt Mine, Southern Poland
Black Moon: November Guest; Nocturne
Brix: Migration
Columbia, A Journal of Literature and Art: Turnpike Vending Machine; Outsider; Return
Controlled Burn: Before Dawn I Leave
Field: Eight Glasses of Water a Day; Good Will Drop-off
Many Mountains Moving: Emergencies; After the Hunt
Salamander: At the Windowsill; Object Permanence; Putting the Dog to Sleep; Crossing; Counting
The Journal: More Than Pity; Nests; Late Summer, Anniversary of My Father's Death
The Marlboro Review: Bugs
The Massachusetts Review: Giselle; Giving Head
West Crook Review: A Single Mother Walks
"Object Permanence" appeared in the anthology *A Map of Hope: Women Writers and Human Rights in the World*, Marjorie Agosin, Editor, Rutger's University Press, New Jersey, 1998.

Special thanks to the Massachusetts Cultural Council Artist Grants Program for their support.

With gratitude, always, to the loves of my life: Jay, Max and Raisa; to Maria, Michael for their constant grace; to Tessa and Peter, Roman Borysthen-Tkacz, Dorothy and Julie Pollack, Michele Hoffman, Russ Sully and Nancy Mitchell (in *all* shared lives) for their many blessings; to Gary Duehr, Heather McHugh, Martha Rhodes, and Chase Twichell for their giving friendships and editorial help on these poems at various stages; to Karen O'Donnell-Leach for eighteen life-sustaining years; and last but not least, to Brittainy Page Heitzman for playing *Stop Doggie Stop* for hours with my children so that these poems could be written.

Publication of this book is supported by a grant from the Pennsylvania Council on the Arts.

Contents

For my mother, Tamara Orlowsky

what was left behind
still waits for the proper signal

It could be the erratic neighing of the night
outside, below the window,

— Miroslav Holub
(tr. Stuart Friebert and Dana Habova)

Prologue

Before Dawn I Leave

with one breath.
Outside, a horse kicks her metal pail.
Someone calls a wrong number.
My sister waves good-bye
at the front door.
I'm draped in a white sheet.
Two young men are careful
not to tilt the stretcher too far
down the front steps.
No one salutes.
Prescriptions expire.
Father's opened leather medical bag stays,
but the sedatives disappear,
as will the money, the house,
the dog, too hysterical and hyperactive
to take along.
Mother strips the bed.
She'll have none of that.

I

November Guest

When I turn toward my reflection
in the window, this woman

lipless, always cold,
for whom, as for me, the wood-burning stove

carefully stacked with sticks
blazes up then dies.

I don't like her.

At the curtain,
edge of house meets edge of yard.

A lamp curves toward the floor —
arched neck, a lack of winter grazing.

Even dust looks starved.

I slide the dishwasher rack out:
a single fork.

Where are the guests
hungry for dinner?

Come, sit down, I tell her.
I'll put in another, stronger bulb.

We can talk,
survive the rain.

Let's pop open some fresh dough.
Together, we can watch it

seep out of its canister —
a slug of goodness, single-celled.

Feather

A feather, its bird, the color red.
All three, like their silence, belong to this day.
Inside this house, at the sink,
a drop of water
immense as sky, immense as itself.
Long shadows stretch across the back yard,
cut borders into afternoon-long provinces,
meager grasses.
Something passed here long before
I stepped into light.
A single feather, its lost script.
Which world, trembling, did it finally choose?

Interminable

A single light's beam
splits the room:
fire's opulent cities.

Opened, a perfume bottle
holds its breath.
Hand mirror, face down,
why do *you* laugh?

...

Then darkness —
a star disintegrated
behind trees,

passengers dropping one-by-one,
their hit mouths
opening the ground.

My reading lamp switched off, snapped
between my fingertips
like a waterfowl's
thin neck —

...

Hard swallow,
one curtainless window —

Objects move from my room:
chair freed from chair,
sure knot of my husband's tie
exits for work.

In the mirror, endless
winter rooms against the wall —
one white body, mine;
the others, stirring.

Nocturne

I listen for things unsettled —
a branch fallen from its tree,

wind's broken compass needle.
Some dog's hoarse bark

marks a neighborhood
yet to be built,

craters dug by bulldozers.
In the garage, raccoons

tilt the lid
off our garbage can,

drag split coffee filters
to the road.

How long can the woodpile
endure its ax?

How long can winter gales endure
a birdhouse's small round door?

The children's slide
turns into ice.

In the bathroom, my cupped hand
lifts my reflection

to my face.
Across a spoon

left on the kitchen counter
skims the thin skin

of my girl's warmed milk.
I listen for things unsettled.

Then sleep, footprints in snow.

And Let Spill

Empty vessel pours empty vessel

—Anonymous, Ukrainian

Glass one I fill
with myself

Glass two I fill
with itself

It will always call me back
to the bare table

A third
I leave alone

It will never break
There are more

Some marked small
One a dark green

I fill with my mother's
aging voice

carry out to the grass
and let spill

I hear her
It's no use

how empty
how empty inside

More Than Pity

The dog officer calls again.

This threat of an empty kennel,
choke collars hung slack
from the hat rack,

last clumps of shit
shovel-flung into the woods
like dead birds,

leaves me in terror.

I admit it was loneliness
more than pity
that called out —

two dogs cowering by the river:
one's lazy as a bowl, the other barks

straight into wind,

into the old woman, self-diagnosed,
terminal, next door

who phones in her complaint,
every afternoon —

the cop, a disc jockey
to whom she requests her song.

Late Summer, Anniversary of My Father's Death

Nothing touches me here. Not the stained glass,
explosive shards of sunlight fallen

short of the pews.
The priest raises his hands, but even God

can't help him get the name right: *Miroslaus*.
He pauses, then hesitantly voices: "Myra..."

Surely a mistake, he thinks, perhaps
his own tired eyes...

He's not from this community.
Arms still raised before his congregation,

he casts shadows
as he sees fit.

On the other side of the room,
an open window, glass lamb

separated at its knees,
parking lot revealed

and a 1975 Volvo; one-third car,
two-thirds Nativity Scene,

my father resurrects
as a severed landscape

into which small loudspeakers
herd their words: *dignity, everlasting*.

Yet I remember no grace.
There was only Mother

and his dead weight and outside
the empty porch,

black June bug mad in its world.

Giselle

If only death came as gracefully to me —
a forest of doctors, backlit,
my grave, a modest table.

My family would weep.
This would be their only role.

They would weep long after
the hospital rooms had been taken down —
corridor props, brooms, steel benches.

They would become their own gnarled cross.
If darkness alone (without chorus) came to raise me,

a tremor through my water glass, my sleeping pill.

Object Permanence

Even a grave can be bulldozed
to give up what it hides.

For years Grandmother saved her money.
Yet when her brother's remains

arrived, she may for all she knew
have been crying

into the bones of a large dog.

...

Father may seem dead
but it's you that's changed.

That sheet placed over his body —
his stillness,

were all just to fool you.
You're the child again,

and the game is to test you,
to see how well you remember.

You lift the sheet, cry out.
Each time his face is locked

into another.
Each time he shows you how

he never left.

...

When my son cries
I lift a napkin over my face,

a paper plate or
a fly swatter.

He stops crying.
He can see me through the swatter.

He knows I'll come back.

II

Circle

Each scar on each tree
without light, without water.
The day is over.

Against the floor,
a chair scrapes hard.

Into bowls,
an avalanche of cereal.
Someone slams the door.

Abruptly into their cabinets,
dishes are stacked.
No one must speak.

Hearts circle like dogs,
afraid of air, of what it carries
from greater distances.

No one must open windows
diligently, methodically closed.

Outsider

1.

English stuck in my throat,
Mrs. Longbone's tobacco breath
lingered over me, her finger
jerking across the page
dragging something on a leash.

2.

My parents were immigrants, not me
who had a penny first given
then taken away
for every English word
spoken in the house.

They gave it instead to the bank:
a large ceramic Dalmatian —
happy wide dog tongue,
opulent black dots.

3.

So many of us in that school room
and one window —
black asphalt,
a single unconjugatable declaration of weeds.

4.

What a relief to be excused
to clean blackboard erasers,
switch on the boiler room vacuum,
covering its bristled mouth
with my hand.
I'd wait for it to wheeze
an angry high pitch.
Then I'd let go.

After the Hunt

The buck's horns were so incipient
I could feel their ache —
bone through flesh, into air.
My sister and I took turns petting the warm body,
as though it were a horse, as though
it could be cut loose from the tree
for us to ride, together.
Nights, after the table was cleared,
we watched Father's Super-8 film
shot from the rifle barrel of the projector.
How thrilling to be blood-tied
to immortal men, seeing each one
reassure the other with a slap on the back,
a Ford station wagon so white
we called it an ambulance.

Blind Man

Father placed a hundred dollars in the collection basket.
Only the priest (at my father's request)
knew who put it there.
Each time he drove past the church
he'd slow down, make the sign of the cross.
When Mother close freedom
instead of him, I wouldn't eat.
Father had my stomach x-rayed
then arranged a courtesy x-ray one month later —
maybe it was the drive together he needed.
"Women are blind," he said,
"but God sees everything."

Counting

My mother kept count of two things:
the number of dogs she put to sleep,
the number of men she thought she had sex with.
She was always wrong. She put more dogs
to sleep than she was willing to remember.
There was always suffering, the incurable
sudden and absolute lack of hunger.
Men seemed to escape her.
She'd hold five fingers up, start counting,
go on to the other hand, get confused
and start again.

Their War

I hated my dolls —
long-legged ones dagger-precise,
wild-haired naked ones that made a broader bruise,
dolls Grandmother and Mother threw,
screaming at each other: "Whore!"
It didn't matter that I lay
on the floor, curled into myself,
my heart a primitive drum.
Each claimed to know more —
the old world a pinched nerve
on the back of Mother's neck.
Each one claimed
to have started over:
my mother, a pinwheel
spinning out of control,
Grandmother slamming her purse
hard on the floor.
It broke open like a piñata —
one piece of candy, some spare change.

Giving Head

When Mother *gave head*, to her it meant
sharing what's on your mind,
her English so broken,
I could imagine the rubble,
the few sealed marked jars
in her throat's basement.

She *gave head*
to the gas station attendant
who drew the dip stick checking its tip,
to the priest who advised her:
"Life is a journey - "
his own worn shoes, a pair of oxen.

She even *gave head* to women —
to the cosmetician who listened
rotating her plexi case,
lipsticks displayed in rows like bullets,
who understood loneliness and stray hairs,
each week offering my mother
a new sliver of color to take home,
twisting the tube erect,
dragging it across her wrist.

After a while, to whom or what hardly mattered.
Stones, meadows, stray dogs,
all seemed to know her.
Fog caressed her, the moon emptied
its massive head like a bucket.

Except her daughter.
When she tried to *give head* to her daughter,
I gave back part of it, the lip —
I was steady as an executioner,
demonstrating my own obscenities.

After that, I don't know
to what non English-speaking corner
she sentenced herself,

her now barely visible hand waving to me,
not so much a good-bye, as a curse.

Wieliczka Salt Mine, Southern Poland

What lives, dies — but deep in its cavern
of vaulted roofs and timber
where without clear exits
a rat couldn't survive,

there would be a cure.
The miners had carved the salt statue
carefully — a large yellowing
tooth-shaped Virgin,

hands pressed together
into a steady flame.
Grandmother believed in the mine —
her own lungs, fractured

blackened chandeliers.
Once, there were horses,
subterranean stables,
wagons to cart the dying

to underground chambers.
Grandmother died next to her tub,
bath salts spilled onto the floor —
packet, slit.

Unclaimed, her miracle re-enters
Wieliczka's black salt,
the hungry pockets of tourists.
What lives, dies.

Today the Salt Mine Brass Band
looks for new material —
Dixieland jazz, easy
military hits.

On Sundays you can see them
above ground, collecting kopeks —
black uniforms, black pillar hats,
red plumes spurting.

Burial

I wouldn't place my rose.
Mother tossed her dirt,
disappointed in love, in a man
who promised always to be there,
and yet now was already
lowered into the ground.

I can't rest my head on his lap,
let him place, even in dreams,
his fingertips on my hair.
That afternoon my sister and I
were twins in black dresses,
two crows hedging toward the grave.
The hole was cut precise as a box,
perhaps by back-hoe...

Nailed shut, the coffin promised
to keep everything out,
preserve only death —
Father powdered until barely familiar —
his expression as if suddenly
he saw someone he loved.

Emergencies

1.

Maybe it was surviving our father,
a river gone dry,

his clothes packed for Good Will,
a suede cap releasing hornets,

or the dog (kept) coddled
like a human turned dog —

splinters of horse's hoofs, smoke-flavored knots
strewn in the back yard.

2.

Maybe it was the war or surviving a war,
Father not coming back,

or the small dog wrapped like a baby
in a nightgown and rocked,

Mother's hysteria, bulging vein,
large, large useless —

3.

At night, we stare at the answering machine's
oval red eye, we wait.

Around our rooms, shadows like horses
gallop and fall —

necks abruptly twisted, their riders
skillful in the art.

4.

Maybe it was the war or the dog
Mother takes to bed

like a piece of burning coal.
At night, she dreams of Father.

He answers her,
forgives her for living, so long, without him.

By morning the powder of her face
fills with blood.

III

Crossing

It's true I unnerve easily
and lately think of squirrels as rats,

as I do anything small
that appears when least expected.

Not my children. I love my children.
And I wonder with what love

they come to my bed every morning
and gently shake me, unafraid —

my face: (I can only imagine),
not unlike a dead squirrel's — teeth clenched

in abbreviated terror — until
untangled from my own skeletal parts,

I find their mother.
Eventually, for them, there will be

only one short semi-circular driveway
leading out, leading in.

Waking

The room re-enters
through a needle.
A medical bag (the doctor long dead)
cracks open like a large walnut.
Outside, fog —
expired day.
A glass of water
guards its own horizon.
From across the floor
a nurse barks:
Let her sleep.
Will I ever learn
to be that still —
obscure name typed
beneath a motionless river,
antiseptic
speared hand?

Case Study: *You are a Woman Carrying a Fetus
    Destined to Become a Famous Violinist*

and that should be reason enough,
the study concludes,

to admit life
for what it is —

a heartbeat set *allegro
molto appassionato,*

translucent fingers
already curled to hold a bow.

Now, by contrast, imagine an accordion player
attached to your umbilical chord.

Simple Sepp expanding
and contracting his huge lung,

arms outstretched as if to hold the universe.
That's personhood — no manicuring of nails,

no receiving the elite,
no ultrasonic notes

so sweet no one dares breathe —
Sepp will come barreling out,

squeezed into an already
rotating world.

Most of us got here that way,
not because of talent —

but strong-fisted,
helmet-first.

Changing Table

He will be a hard worker.
I lift his legs —
Could they really be that frail?
Everyone's afraid to clean the tiny penis.
My husband become father becomes invisible,
his briefcase heavier than stone.
Trees splinter against the sky;
we cannot rock him hard enough,
feed him fast enough.
In the kitchen, small drops of milk warm my wrist.
I wait for the house to grow quiet.
Cries erupt from upstairs.
A child becomes family.

Turbulence

In my lap, a map of the world
split and flattened, nobody spared.
Where is the face of a woman who's suffered enough,
her ill son pointing past this dream? —
the face of the steward,
calming, benign
who in a previous life
could've been a drop of water.
The bathroom door swings open, vacant.
Thunder booms above a field.
I open my eyes.
Familial faces drop before me like oxygen masks.
In the flash before death,
who inside of me would scream the loudest?

A Single Mother Walks

the room's periphery
shaking an empty maraca.
Her daughter does not follow her,
does not clink the triangle
handed to her out of all the broken
instruments spilled onto the floor.
She is drawn to the sink,
to a tray of watercolors
she holds under the running faucet.
She'll hold it there
until her hands are free
of their captive black river,
until bled from each whole oval,
the colors come clean.

Mirror

Who is this woman, eager for a tip,
who tells me *next time go darker* —

Does she think: *old woman*
as she bends over me

carefully placing my neck
in the groove of the sink?

Does she struggle for conversation
the air stale between us

hoping maybe this time,
eyes closed, I won't answer,

waiting for the deepest black to take.

Bugs

Scratching, her children are at last occupied.

The mosquito she smashed
with a newspaper

left so much blood, she thought
she'd killed a relative.

How negligent,
these breeding grounds

left unattended —
inflatable pool, the bird bath scum

so thick it smells.
Everywhere.

From a tree branch, caterpillars
like furry intestines

spill out of a cloth beach bag
left hanging overnight.

Summer has left her
feeling ill, rubbing

the palms of her hands.
Her children don't even look like her.

Migration

We planned to drive cross-country,
instead I sit at the kitchen table
watching dust balls blow across the apartment.
They are their own temporary webs.
Sweeping them is like sweeping sea foam,
or lifting clouds.
They gather with their own strength,
weave the slightest of threads.
Who ever tried tearing one apart?
There are families of them
under beds, washed up against barriers,
a shoe, an empty boat
with oars missing —
No sign of a survivor for days.

Offering

Dogs lie devoured,
curled into their own meanness,

sedated by what was eaten
and then rid of, they need nothing.

Out on the porch, a water bowl freezes.
It waits for the thud of my boot.

I gather towels, nightgowns,
wait for it to get colder.

In a corner of my kitchen, framed
within opened cabinet doors,

a news reporter clutches a mike,
excited by the sound of his own voice.

Around him, white flurry.
I leave one house to kneel outside,

push warm gifts into other dark houses.
The dogs wake, know my smell.

Their eyes catch fire.

Inside

I check my closet every night.

Is that shoe a foot?

Is that hat a head?

Are those sleeves, arms?

The scarf a noose?

Umbrella a knife?

Is anyone inside?

I check my closet every night.

Geography

Who did we forget to call?
How long have we been sleeping?
Outside, clothespins cluster on a line.
Was it once a river instead, this conversation
we work too hard at, tired, in front of the flicker
of someone's murder?

Blood grows tired where it travels.
Useless to us at the end of the day,
at the table, your keys sprawl heavy
as our hands, so exhausted our lives
around which we close borders
from everything we've sworn to love.

At the Windowsill

Insect leg, soft splinter.
Too much lead paint.
The storm window's guillotine, opened.
A white curtain's cloudy stain.
On the other side?

Long glance to a rose bush,
to that neighboring pear tree,
its bright green hanging sack
where all afternoon
Japanese beetles drop

like pieces of broken glass.
They give up last petals
to send their bodies flying —
warm, downwind scent,
strip of poison, blossoming.

IV

Return

- FW

We love to return
to these streets, trees.
The occupants of the white house
we once lived in
(barely recognizable)
look pulseless
out on the porch swing —
the way we imagine
we would've eventually looked
had we stayed.
Here our coronation begins.
Where, after, do we turn,
dragging our pelts behind?
Where is that car overturned
killing the teenagers
on the way to the rock concert?
We were never that popular.
Yet, at the town's cemetery,
the dead are eager.
See the one with the hat?
See the one holding the stone?
There are more.
A breeze arrives from another
unmarked town, vacant acres,
a few cows tacked in place.
We love to come home for a visit,
look nervously at our watches —
our brilliant lives
so far ahead of us
they've already been claimed.

On Empty, the Car Continues to Drive

Past unnamed streets,
the wind elbowing through —
past the single shopper pushing her cart,
past a bank teller's window,
the red button that sends the canister far, far away...
past the child's ball bouncing in front of a car
like a ravenous dog
past hunger,
the bound river neither north or south,
past the one horse in traffic —
its terrified eye that I pass, rider deep in her seat .

Turnpike Vending Machine

Pocket-knife-corkscrew-fork ensemble
outfitting even the smallest breakdown,
I want you,

your dangers fanned out, displayed,
graceful utility, poised
as a hummingbird —

hormone on a slim chain,
I ache to close,
put to bed.

Who thought they understood me well enough
to suggest sex
for a quarter —

a vinyl rain bonnet
meticulously folded,
a single gargle of mouthwash,

that scarlet dress I haven't yet bought
but wear as skin — all those, available here,
multi-colored spools of thread

and compact needles
I'll need to maintain it.
Take my money,

though I have none,
spent on family,
my daughter asleep in the car,

my son full as a tick
on Snapple.
Even so,

extra money should provide extra options:
a rabbit's foot, well-manicured;
a spare chess piece,

queen — just in case
luck turns,
hungry, greasy, looking for you.

Good Will Drop-off

Overwhelmingly generous, this doll's head
(eyes rolled upward) lying next to black ice skates,

loosely laced, lumpy at the ankles, chipped blades.
Whoever donated these cared that someone inherit them

to fall through ice. I should take them.
I should be Oksana Baiul.

This would please the strangers
who — hopeful, blind — stop to tell me

there is a resemblance. Kind, absent-minded
strangers with too much time, lonely

for talk, abandoned by their dogs
for the stronger street-ripe smell of trash.

I'd like to meet the anonymous donors.
After hours they pull up in their station wagons

to drop their load in the gray snow.
How free each one must feel driving away —

flat empty purses, records without jackets,
just the left shoe...

Is this as good as we get in giving —
accumulated, worn, stripped, tossed

shrouds drained of color — one
with a truck to fill by next morning,

picking through, thinking — someone, someone
can use this.

Eight Glasses of Water a Day

Where do they go
if not out through the body and eventually,
miraculously, back to earth.

Nothing drowns beneath skin,
everything surfaces like snakes
out pores,

the body's crawl spaces
pungent with fear
and love.

It's good, they tell me,
this cleansing.
Imagine a hose

always full, left on.
Imagine a rhododendron
in a forest,

explosion of color —
after rain,
after surrender.

A man could still love me,
a face soft as a nun's,
decades of poison

released.
I want to live longer
so that I can drink

more, excusing myself
quietly from every room.
Let me die

preoccupied —
fires extinguished,
a steady rowing backwards.

Nests

Hinged on a black branch,
empty when I find them,

they remind me of what killed you,
of what couldn't be coughed away.

When do birds nest?
When night claims everything,
holds it with its claw?

What impulse spreads their wings
across the hollow skulls of eggs?

Buoyant in entanglement,
I call anything that warms me a nest.

Putting the Dog to Sleep

He hates the way I smell —
too clean, carrying groceries in,

and I hate
but continue to feed him.

I remember the perfume I wore to pick out my dog,
organizing my wallet, vacuuming the car seats,

waiting until that right one appeared,
faster than others

from under a dark and moldering porch.
Bare-chested, a boy greeted me holding a dead snake.

He didn't care that I tried calling earlier,
his own mother out for a while...

Today, a tricycle lies turned on its side
just at the woods.

I've gotten older
and my dog's teeth, brown with neglect.

He gets fatter, blacker, more skittish
as I pull my children closer.

I know I'll do it —
while they're in school

or not.
They see me at the back door

watching,
too nervous to keep anything nervous alive.

Outlet, Fork, and Phone

Floor curves into a grin.
It likes the dead cat's white fur still as air,

swept across his upholstered chair.
Bedroom closet opens its doors

to suits cut for a dwarf,
was it before or after the illness,

after bad news, after he fell inside himself?
Who knew he would end like this —

a slender hand coming up bare
no gold, no gracious dove,

no glossy black hat,
just Mother in the kitchen

stacking cans for the cat.
Which is my room, is it this —

a bed too big, more mine now than his?
As the table, mirror, stove:

Who will take care of me when I grow old?
Not the outlet, or the fork, or the phone.

Rendezvous

What good was your shaving?
The clock slices night
into pieces too small to eat.
We cajole, promise what we don't have.
Our sumptuous evening grows cold.
What good was your shaving?
At the toilet, our daughter needs wiping,
our son, proud of his — *a bus out-of-control,*
an angry dot-to-dot.
They could talk about it forever.
What good was your shaving?
Your razor still wet.
Over and over we wash hands.

The Curtain's Borders

Knuckles knock hard in the dark,
the luck of wood a bad assumption;

whole mirrors, even worse.
Someone stays, drinks from a cracked cup.

Voices carry from woods,
move through my hands

to place a crimson vase on the table.
What fills it?

Each winter, what will not sleep
escapes, stirred-up,

keys spilled — returns.
Rooms grow small.

What do I keep if not myself?
The curtain's borders —

Outside, looking back,
unanticipated day,

A dry well,
afternoon heat —

my family carrying water, blades of tall grass
for our dead.

I'm not among them on their temporary hill.

1975
The Living and the Dead, Ann Hayes
In the Face of Descent, T. Alan Broughton

1976
The Week the Dirigible Came, Jay Meek
Full of Lust and Good Usage, Stephen Dunn

1977
How I Escaped from the Labyrinth and Other Poems, Philip Dacey
The Lady from the Dark Green Hills, Jim Hall
For Luck: Poems 1962-1977, H.L. Van Brunt
By the Wreckmaster's Cottage, Paula Rankin

1978
New & Selected Poems, James Bertolino
The Sun Fetcher, Michael Dennis Browne
A Circus of Needs, Stephen Dunn
The Crowd Inside, Elizabeth Libbey

1979
Paying Back the Sea, Philip Dow
Swimmer in the Rain, Robert Wallace
Far from Home, T. Alan Broughton
The Room Where Summer Ends, Peter Cooley
No Ordinary World, Mekeel McBride

1980
And the Man Who Was Traveling Never Got Home, H.L. Van Brunt
Drawing on the Walls, Jay Meek
The Yellow House on the Corner, Rita Dove
The 8-Step Grapevine, Dara Wier
The Mating Reflex, Jim Hall

1981
A Little Faith, John Skoyles
Augers, Paula Rankin
Walking Home from the Icehouse, Vern Rutsala
Work and Love, Stephen Dunn
The Rote Walker, Mark Jarman
Morocco Journal, Richard Harteis
Songs of a Returning Soul, Elizabeth Libbey

1988
Preparing to Be Happy, T. Alan Broughton
Red Letter Days, Mekeel McBride
The Abandoned Country, Thomas Rabbitt
The Book of Knowledge, Dara Wier
Changing the Name to Ochester, Ed Ochester
Weaving the Sheets, Judith Root

1989
Recital in a Private Home, Eve Shelnutt
A Walled Garden, Michael Cuddihy
The Age of Krypton, Carol J. Pierman
Land That Wasn't Ours, David Keller
Stations, Jay Meek
The Common Summer: New and Selected Poems, Robert Wallace
The Burden Lifters, Michael Waters
Falling Deeply into America, Gregory Djanikian

1990
Why the River Disappears, Marcia Southwick
Staying Up For Love, Leslie Adrienne Miller
Dreamer, Primus St. John

1991
Permanent Change, John Skoyles
Clackamas, Gary Gildner
Tall Stranger, Gillian Conoley
The Gathering of My Name, Cornelius Eady
A Dog in the Lifeboat, Joyce Peseroff
Raised Underground, Renate Wood
Divorce: A Romance, Paula Rankin

1992
Modern Ocean, James Harms
The Astonished Hours, Peter Cooley
You Won't Remember This, Michael Dennis Browne
Twenty Colors, Elizabeth Kirschner
First A Long Hesitation, Eve Shelnutt
Bountiful, Michael Waters
Blue for the Plough, Dara Wier
All That Heat in a Cold Sky, Elizabeth Libbey

1993
Trumpeter, Jeannine Savard
Cuba, Ricardo Pau-Llosa
The Night World and the Word Night, Franz Wright
The Book of Complaints, Richard Katrovas

1994
If Winter Come: Collected Poems, 1967–1992, Alvin Aubert
Of Desire and Disorder, Wayne Dodd
Ungodliness, Leslie Adrienne Miller
Rain, Henry Carlile
Windows, Jay Meek
A Handful of Bees, Dzvinia Orlowsky

1995
Germany, Caroline Finkelstein
Housekeeping in a Dream, Laura Kasischke
About Distance, Gregory Djanikian
Wind of the White Dresses, Mekeel McBride
Above the Tree Line, Kathy Mangan
In the Country of Elegies, T. Alan Broughton
Scenes from the Light Years, Anne C. Bromley
Quartet, Angela Ball

1996
Back Roads, Patricia Henley
Dyer's Thistle, Peter Balakian
Beckon, Gillian Conoley
The Parable of Fire, James Reiss
Cold Pluto, Mary Ruefle
Orders of Affection, Arthur Smith
Colander, Michael McFee

1997
Growing Darkness, Growing Light, Jean Valentine
Selected Poems, 1965-1995, Michael Dennis Browne
Your Rightful Childhood: New and Selected Poems, Paula Rankin
Headlands: New and Selected Poems, Jay Meek
Soul Train, Allison Joseph
The Autobiography of a Jukebox, Cornelius Eady
The Patience of the Cloud Photographer, Elizabeth Holmes
Madly in Love, Aliki Barnstone
An Octave Above Thunder: New and Selected Poems, Carol Muske

1998
Yesterday Had a Man in It, Leslie Adrienne Miller
Definition of the Soul, John Skoyles
Dithyrambs, Richard Katrovas
Postal Routes, Elizabeth Kirschner
The Blue Salvages, Wayne Dodd
The Joy Addict, James Harms
Clemency, Colette Inez
Scattering the Ashes, Jeff Friedman
Sacred Conversations, Peter Cooley
Life Among the Trolls, Maura Stanton

1999
Justice, Caroline Finkelstein
Edge of House, Dzvinia Orlowsky
A Thousand Friends of Rain: New & Selected Poems 1976-1998, Kim Stafford
The Devil's Child, Fleda Brown Jackson
World as Dictionary, Jesse Lee Kercheval
Vereda Tropical, Ricardo Pau-Llosa
The Museum of the Revolution, Angela Ball
Our Master Plan, Dara Wier